Rosemary M Chileshe

I0201909

THE FRUITS OF THE ONE WHO COUNSELS

The 9 Attributes of The Holy Spirit

Swanilenga®

Swanilenga® Publications London

DEDICATION

This book is dedicated to EVERYONE, everywhere on every level in their Spiritual Journey. I hope as a Believer in Christ, the content stirs up / renews your excitement in recognising the 9 attributes of The Holy Spirit residing in you and I hope in turn, that encourages you to monitor the growth of the various attributes on a daily basis as you continue to soak in the word and to remain hungry for THE ONE WHO COUNSELS. If you have not yet come to Christ, I hope you get the desire to seek Him more and accept Him as your Lord and Saviour and in turn, begin to enjoy everything the Holy Spirit represents. Remember, in order for you to recognise & operate in the Fruits of The Holy Spirit as referenced in Galatians 5:22-25, you need to have received the outpouring of The Holy Spirit as referenced in Acts 1:8.

CONTENTS

ACKNOWLEDGMENTS

I continue to PRAISE & GLORIFY The Triune God (Our Father), Jesus Christ (The Son, Our Lord and Saviour) and of course, the reason for this book, The Holy Spirit (The One who Counsels). In ALL things, with God is my heart, I am forever thankful. I would also like to say a SUPER big thank you to ALL my family for their continued support and to my contributors, listed in the order of the fruits they have contributed on; **Ruthy Chileshe**; **Mabel Nalishuwa, Denise Jacobsen, Lunnetta Ale, Helen Nanjira Gregory, Sarah Hombarume**, **Kasia Zarczynska**, **Patricia Nalishuwa** and **Suzanne Chileshe**. My back cover profile image is from a photoshoot I helped put together, themed; The Beauty of Enchanted Woods. Credits go to; **Albert St Clair** (Photographer), **Karen Salandy** (Make Up Artist) & **B Jablonska** (Hair Stylist)

Rosemary M Chileshe

i

INTRODUCTION

Hello there, REJOICING for this is my 2ND Book!! Writing it was always going to happen through God's grace and guidance. The first moment He blessed with the seed to write *Embracing Number 7* was the moment He poured into my Spirit the desire to continue writing however many books as I feel led to write. I love nothing more than moving on ordered steps.

Coming up with the title of this book and theme took a series of prayers. In everything I do I always want to ensure it is done in line with God's will so that means, a lot of time and patience committed in my prayers, quiet time and seeking God's direction on what to write about, how to theme the chapters and the whole book collectively and of course, what to call it. By July 2014 (7 months after my first book had been published) I already knew this book would be themed around *The Fruits of The Holy Spirit* in line with **Galatians 5:22-25** but the title would not be so specific, so off I went and started writing down titles centred around that and for every title I wrote down I committed it into prayer and after a while in my quiet time, I made a note of what I was discerning regarding the proposed title. Finally! like a deposit made into my heart, the title was birthed and a book cover was instructed with the Main Title; **THE FRUITS OF THE ONE WHO COUNSELS** and Sub Title; The 9 Attributes of The Holy Spirit

In the last 2 years, I have really grown in my understanding of The Holy Spirt and how He operates in me. The subject scripture in this book is; **Galatians 5:22-25 (NLT)**[22] *But the Holy Spirit produces this kind of fruit in our lives: love, joy, peace,* *patience, kindness, goodness, faithfulness, [23] gentleness, and self-control. There is no law against these things![24] Those who belong to Christ Jesus have nailed the passions and desires of their sinful nature to his cross and crucified them there. [25] Since we are living by the Spirit, let us follow the Spirit's leading in every part of our lives.*

When you read what I reference as my life's blueprint; The Bible and when you soak in God's word, you realise there are many other scriptures where the Holy Spirit is referenced. Here is another, which fits in nicely with my theme and book cover; **Luke 3:21-22 (MSG)** *After all the people were baptized, Jesus was baptized. As he was praying, the sky opened up and the Holy Spirit, like a dove descending, came down on him. And along with the Spirit, a voice: "You are my Son, chosen and marked by my love, pride of my life.*

A question which may spring to your mind right now, could be; why that title? Firstly, I do not claim to know everything about The Holy Spirit, so this book is written from a personal perspective and how I relate and interact with the 9 attributes and on the other angle, what the 9 attributes mean to my 9 contributors.

On that note!:) enjoy, feel free to write down your thoughts on pages I have deliberately left blank for you as you navigate through.

1

LOVE

The FIRST fruit is LOVE, what is it and what does it mean to others? Here is what my 1ST contributor had to say;

True love is painful and sacrificial yet beautiful. Jesus suffered painfully to redeem us from our sin because of the true great love our Father has for us. John 3;16. Love is about taking an extra mile and also doing the above and beyond. God demonstrated His love for all of us by sacrificing his only beloved son to die in our place for the sins that we have. Now if that is not love then what is?

Love comes with forgiveness and endurance, it is selfless, a feeling for the other – not an easy thing but encouraging to know that countless people in this world do it and truly live out God's greatest commandment to love God and one another as He has loved us (Matthew 22: 37-40). Love challenges us to get in very difficult and dark places. Love does not choose colour, shape, smell, religion etc. It challenges us to love he very being that causes us so much pain, its unconditional, you can't place conditions to it. Love has so many faces but in this case I talk about a few variations centered on God's love.

Love is free yet is binding. In the words of Catherine Wybourne a Benedictine nun "Love is more easily experienced than defined. In a theological virtue by which we love God above all things and our neighbours as ourselves for His sake, it seems remote until we encounter it enfleshed, so to say, in the life of another – in acts of kindness, generosity and self-sacrifice, love is the one thing that can never hurt anyone, although it may cost dearly. The paradox of love is that it is supremely free yet attaches us with bonds stronger than death. It cannot be bought or sold; there is nothing it cannot face, love is life's free greatest blessing. **RUTHY CHILESHE.**

3

Beautifully contributed. LOVE in The Bible is covered in many different and amazing ways. We know that God is Love, therefore love is from God. **John 3:16** has been referenced above, I love this version of it *"For God so loved (agape) the world, that He gave His only begotten Son, that whoever believes in Him should not perish, but have eternal life"*

The term "agape" represents God's love for us, which is a non-partial and is sacrificial. It is a type of love which requires a relationship with God through our Lord Jesus Christ. Agape love is described as being patient, kind, truthful, unselfish, trusting, believing, hopeful, and enduring. It is not jealous, boastful, arrogant, rude, selfish, or angry. It gives and sacrifices expecting nothing back in return.

One other most referenced scripture on Love, which supports the description of "Agape" above is from **1 Corinthians 13:4-8** *Love is patient, love is kind. It does not envy, it does not boast, it is not proud. It is not rude, it is not self-seeking, it is not easily angered, it keeps no record of wrongs. Love does not delight in evil but rejoices with the truth. It always protects, always trusts, always hopes, always perseveres. Love never fails. Now I know in part; then I shall know fully, even as I am fully known. And now these three remain: faith, hope and love. But the greatest of these is love.*

Love is one of the primary characteristics of God. Likewise, as believers we should recognise that God has equipped us with the capacity for love since we are created in His image. This capacity for love is one of the ways in which we are "created in the image of God." We also know that God's love is unconditional. Personally, I rejoice in God's unconditional love for us and in my personal journey with Him I have grown to understand what loving unconditionally really means in ALL things and in whatever pain I am afflicted with, I have learnt to give love in return. In contrast, where God's love is now operational, the love we give is

THE FRUITS OF THE ONE WHO COUNSELS

usually conditional and based on how other people treat us. This kind of love is based on familiarity and direct interaction, however, God wants us to express agape love.

1 Peter 1:22 states; *You were cleansed from your sins when you obeyed the truth, so now you must show sincere love to each other as brothers and sisters. Love each other deeply with all your heart.*

The Bible teaches us that true love never fails. As Christians we should be encouraged to show unconditional love, which is eternal and to be partakers of God's divine nature. If you have not yet come to Christ, I hope you will open your heart to the prompting of The Holy Spirit and through God's Grace you will desire to remain steadfast and express love as defined in the Bible.

Wikipedia says; *love is a variety of different feelings, states, and attitudes that ranges from interpersonal affection ("I love my mother") to pleasure ("I loved that meal"). It can refer to an emotion of a strong attraction and personal attachment.[1] It can also be a virtue representing human kindness, compassion, and affection—"the unselfish loyal and benevolent concern for the good of another".[2] It may also describe compassionate and affectionate actions towards other humans, one's self or animals.*

I used Wikipedia because a lot of you refer to it for a general definition and I wanted to highlight what most of you can relate to at first thought. In contrast to what Wikipedia says, I believe Christian Love teaches us that love is not just a feeling you get. Instead love is about giving to others and not necessary expecting to receive anything back from them in return. Christian love also represents giving respect to others, being charitable and showing mercy. When we look at Agape love, The Bible shows us that God does not simply love us; He is the perfect description of love. God loves because He is love. He is the characteristic and expression of love.

I am thankful always that even when I do not deserve it, just like He loves you, God loves me too. He showed His love for all of us and He paid the supreme sacrifice for us as the ones He loves and redeemed us on the cross when His son, our Lord and Saviour, Jesus Christ died for our sins. That type of sacrificial love which is not based on mere feelings but by God's spirit and encourages a joyful determination to put the welfare of others above our own does not come naturally to us humans and It is hard for us to follow and to fulfil but we are encouraged by God's word and example to love others with His heart. In The Bible, the parable of the Good Samaritan gives us an example of one type of sacrifice for others.

In most cases living in this society in this timeline, we fall short in our character, therefore we may struggle to show the type of sacrificial love which was shown in the parable of the Good Samaritan. We are encouraged to demonstrate agape love and love as God loves. When we accepted Jesus Christ as our Lord and Saviour and became God's children through the Holy Spirit, agape love got poured into our hearts. **Romans 5:5** *And hope does not put us to shame, because God's love has been poured out into our hearts through the Holy Spirit, who has been given to us.* We must therefore find it easy and a natural instinct to love one another as God loves us.

Romans 12:9-16 *states; Love must be sincere. Hate what is evil; cling to what is good. [10] Be devoted to one another in love. Honor one another above yourselves. [11] Never be lacking in zeal, but keep your spiritual fervor, serving the Lord. [12] Be joyful in hope, patient in affliction, faithful in prayer. [13] Share with the Lord's people who are in need. Practice hospitality. [14] Bless those who persecute you; bless and do not curse. [15] Rejoice with those who rejoice; mourn with those who mourn. [16] Live in harmony with one another. Do not be proud, but be willing to associate with people of low position. Do not be conceited.*

In whatever circumstances you are facing or going through, if you are finding it difficult to love as you should, my hope for you as a new creation in Christ to reach a positon were you seek our Heavenly Father to show you how you can walk, talk and react in love when those around you are doing the opposite. Personally on several occasions I recite and pray **Psalm 139:23-24** *Search me, O God, and know my heart: try me, and know my thoughts* [24] *And see if there be any wicked way in me, and lead me in the way everlasting.*

May you also ask our Heavenly Father to show you what lies in your heart and seek repentance for anything evil. May you come to a place in your heart where you love everyone unconditionally. The final part in **Matthew 5:43-44** states *"But I tell you: Love your enemies and pray for those who persecute you."*

I would like to end with one of my favourite scriptures, one that I have grown to live by. **1 Peter 4:8** *Above all, love each other deeply, because love covers over a multitude of sins.*

Rosemary M Chileshe

2

JOY

The SECOND fruit is JOY, what is it and what does it mean to others? Here is what my 2ND contributor had to say;

JOY AS A FRUIT OF THE SPIRIT...A personal opinion

What is joy? one may ask. My own personal understanding of joy is that it is the outward expression of happiness or contentment that comes from within. In other words, the kind of happiness that does not depend on one's circumstances or experiences. For instance, a person's mood does not get swayed regardless of what they are going through. There are a number of things that could have a negative impact on our mood, such as financial struggles, lack of employment, bad weather conditions etc. As we do not always have control of what life may throw at us, putting all our trust and focus on God is the ultimate source of our joy.

Joy is a choice. Therefore, one can choose to be joyful through all circumstances; good or bad. Moreover, in times when we experience sadness due to circumstances beyond our control, there is assurance in knowing that this only lasts for a season...The scripture tells us that "Weeping may last for a season but joy comes in the morning"...Psalm 30:5.

By being joyful, I believe you have nothing to lose and everything to gain (as the saying goes). There are so many benefits of being joyful; it gives hope, it is a source of healing to the mind, body and soul. Joy also generates a positive energy, therefore people will be drawn to you because of that. In my own personal experience, I've learnt that positive people often attract those with a similar spirit. In addition, having joy automatically eliminates any negative energy such as anxiety or depression that one might have. Naturally, it's impossible to be happy and sad at the same time. In conclusion, God wants us to be joyful always according to scripture in, 1 Thessalonians 5:16. **MABEL NALISHUWA.**

A great opinion shared. Joy means different things to all of us. To some of us, joy is associated with a forced feeling which comes as a result of certain circumstances and to others, joy is seen as a spontaneous and emotional response of the heart. For other groups of people, joy comes from doing certain activities such as socialisng with friends or being in fellowship or from making certain decisions such as a change in lifestyle.

One of the downfalls of forced joy is the temporary results it gives. One best illustration of this is in the parable of the sower; **Matthew 13: 20-21** *The seed on the rocky soil represents those who hear the message and immediately receive it with joy. But since they don't have deep roots, they don't last long. They fall away as soon as they have problems or are persecuted for believing God's word.*

Merely seeking joy by seeking pleasurable excitement does not give us true joy. To experience the best and longest joy, we must seek God's way and yield wholeheartedly to His creative purpose. We must seek God's will not our own.

When we give room to joy which is not rooted in Christ or which does not come from our walk with God, one other reason it only lasts for a short period of time is because when afflictions or persecutions or hard times come, joy quickly disappears because it is not rooted to anything. It is not the fruit of the Spirit; it is not the joy of Christ that delights in God no matter what the external circumstances are.

We see joy illustrated as a wonderful expression in **1 Peter 1:8** *Though you have not seen him, you love him; and even though you do not see him now, you believe in him and are filled with an inexpressible and glorious joy.*

Many scriptures encourages us to find joy or being joyful even in our sad or painful moments. In most times, It is not easy to find joy merely from the flesh but as we live in Christ and walk in His Spirit, the joy we encounter is deeply and firmly rooted even in our painful moments.

Romans 5:3 says, *We can rejoice, too, when we run into problems and trials, for we know that they help us develop endurance.*

2 Corinthians 8:2 says, *They are being tested by many troubles, and they are very poor. But they are also filled with abundant joy, which has overflowed in rich generosity.*

In the above two scriptures, through Apostle Paul's writing, we can see that even in his suffering, he found long lasting joy, which could only be as a result of the fruit of the Holy Spirit. He did not demonstrate superficial joy instead he showed us examples of what deeply and firmly rooted joy looks like.

There are many other scriptures in the Bible, which call us to find long lasting joy produced from the fruit of the Spirit such as in **Matthew 5:12** which says; *"Rejoice and be glad, because great is your reward in heaven, for in the same way they persecuted the prophets who were before you"* And in **Philippians 4:4** which says, *"Rejoice in the Lord always; again I say rejoice!"*

As believers in Christ, we can be encouraged to do as the scriptures call us to do and enjoy the joy in all circumstances by acknowledging that through our own strength we cannot accomplish that joy but through God's Grace, we can. We must cry out to our Heavenly Father and ask for His Holy Spirit to work in us and to produce the fruit of joy in us. If we look to God and set our minds on the higher things and all things biblical, we will experience God's love.

Personally for me, as I continue to walk in Christ and as I soak in the word of God, the joy that I experience as a fruit of The Holy Spirit even in my painful moments is evident as a result of the indwelling Spirit of God, which has the character of Christ's joy. It is not temporary therefore it does not vanish like the dew when the hot sun of affliction rises in the sky.

The scripture in **Isaiah 55:12** *"You will live in joy and peace. The mountains and hills will burst into song and the trees of the field will clap their hands!"* and other scriptures show us that as we yield to God's purpose, we find the key to biblical joy, a fruit of God's Spirit, we will always be uplifted. His joy is greater than any negative circumstance that could occur in our lives.

When we look at biblical joy, we find that it is inseparable from our relationship with God. It comes from our knowledge and understanding of what our purpose in life is. When we allow God to be present in our lives, the joy we experience can be compared to that referenced in **Psalm 16:11** *You make known to me the path of life; you will fill me with joy in your presence, with eternal pleasures at your right hand.*

We also find that biblical joy begins when God calls, we hear His gospel, understand it, believe it and then receive it. Biblical joy is present in our relationship with our Heavenly Father. As we understand more of God and His ways, our walk becomes different to the walk of those with a worldly way of thinking this world because not only do we begin to understand God's overall purpose, we also see it, our eyes of understanding are enlightened. We know we have been forgiven and have a place in His purpose because we now have His Spirit. No more life-changing experience can ever happen to a human-being than when God calls and understanding dawns. It forever alters our perspective on life itself and on the things we formerly trusted to give us satisfaction.

Having joy has been evident in my life that I have a purpose on this earth and that I was born for an ordained reason. As a further revelation of God, scripture tells us in **John 6:44** *"No one can come to me unless the Father who sent me draws them, and I will raise them up at the last day"*. And in **1 Corinthians 2:10** *these are the things God has revealed to us by his Spirit. The Spirit searches all things, even the deep things of God"*

We see from the above two scriptures that no one can come to our Heavenly Father and find the purpose of life unless by His Spirit, He calls them and reveals it to them.

Fellow brothers and sisters in faith, are you experiencing and enjoying the fullness of our Heavenly Father's joy? In His word, we can see that joy is found in His presence and His presence resides in us. As we focus our mind and heart on our Heavenly Father and begin to praise Him for what He has done in our life, joy manifests in us.

As we begin to praise and thank our Heavenly Father, in His presence, we have an opportunity to access the type of joy only He can give. I am a believer that as we have accepted Christ as our Lord and Saviour, our Heavenly Father resides in us wants us to experience His endless supernatural joy and peace at all times, regardless of what circumstances we are facing. That is why in other scripture we are encouraged not to feel discouraged, defeated or burdened for Greater is our

God who lives in us. In Him we have fullness of His joy and we are strengthened.

As we search and desire biblical joy with our whole lives, we honor our Heavenly Father and in turn we are transformed by His Grace and we thus experience the inner joy we cannot fake. The more we approach God for this transformation, the more of God we will encounter.

There is plenty of biblical evidence that Christian joy is not the mere product of the human spirit in response to pleasant circumstances. It is the fruit of God's Spirit. And it is not just a human joy; it is the very joy of Christ fulfilled in us. As you desire to get lasting joy in your heart, may I encourage you to meditate on God's word in line with **Psalm 119:14** *I rejoice in following your statutes as one rejoices in great riches.*

Psalm 19:8 *The precepts of the LORD are right, giving joy in the heart. The commands of the LORD are radiant, giving light to the eyes.*

Being in God's presence – **Psalm 16:9 – 11** *Therefore my heart is glad and my tongue rejoices; my body also will rest secure, because you will not abandon me to the realm of the dead, nor will you let your faithful one see decay. You make known to me the path of life; you will fill me with joy in your presence, with eternal pleasures at your right hand.*

As we look deeper into what the Bible tells us about joy, we find as a fruit of the Holy Spirit, joy comes from God. It was created in the character of God and it was born in the person of our Lord Jesus Christ.

The ability for us to find that joy comes from our walk with God, through His Holy Spirit. In **Psalm 68:3** we read; *"But* *may the righteous be glad and rejoice before God; may they be happy and joyful"*

As we seek more of God's presence and remain obedient to His word and we stay in tune with the prompting of His Spirit, our joy increases too.

3

PEACE

The THIRD fruit is PEACE, what is it and what does it mean to others? Here is what my 3RD contributor had to say;

> *Peace to me is a feeling of inner tranquility, a sense of quietness and a chance to just be. I feel it can also be used to end disputes by finding peace and calm with each other. Peace is also the sound of birds singing in the morning, the sun shining on my face, the sounds of waves crashing on an empty beach.. the appreciation of the beautifulness that surrounds us. Peace is the acceptance of oneself and an understanding of others. Peace can also come from the quiet moments of prayer, when your heart is focused on wanting to spread goodness and love. Love is also Peace. The ability to love is the ability to find and spread Peace.* **DENISE JACOBSEN.**

Another great contribution and we see both love and peace as the fruits of the Spirit interlinking.

Being peaceful or at peace is what all of us want in life, however only a few seem to find peace which comes as a fruit of the Spirit. When we look at the meaning of peace, "harmony" comes to mind or as contributed above, "tranquility." Like with the other fruits, what "peace" means to me will be different to what it means to you depending on what circumstances we are facing. Sometimes many experience a false sense of peace, whilst others experience an inner peace, which can only be connected to the peace God gives.

John 14:27 *Peace I leave with you; my peace I give you. I do not give to you as the world gives. Do not let your hearts be troubled and do not be afraid.*

In the above scripture, the peace our Lord Jesus has given to us enables us to be calm and to be still in all that we face. We see that we have been left with His peace, which we must

19

take hold of. We must receive it and apply it our lives. The peace of God does not promise us that trouble will not come but instead it encourages us that whatever we encounter, we are not to be troubled nor to feel defeated, we should feel calm with untroubled hearts.

In the above scripture, we also see a type of positive peace, which is settled in its own strength and is not intimated by circumstances.

If you find your heart is troubled, check that you are not doubting God's word. Ensure you are at a place in your life where you are believing Him and trusting His promise of peace.

One reason why you may have a troubled heart could be due to anxiety which arises from your past / present circumstances which may not even be in your control. You may worry about things that may / not happen. Our Heavenly Father promises to supply our future needs. Be encouraged by His work in; **Matthew 6:34** *Therefore do not worry about tomorrow, for tomorrow will worry about itself. Each day has enough trouble of its own.*

Although the peace which God gives us is valuable, many still give room to a sense of false peace. Their search for peace only serves as an attempt to get away from their problems. As a result, many people seek peace through other avenues such as alcohol, drugs and all other things worldly. We must be mindful that without God at the core of our lives, we cannot find any real peace in this world. The sense of false peace will only result in temporary joy.

When we speak of peace, sometimes it can be perceived in a negative way. As an example, most people believe their experience of peace is only evident because they have no signs of conflict. Having the peace of God should confirm an active fellowship and harmony with God. We should see peace as a blessing which should be desired and enjoyed by all.

The peace we see in the Bible reflects the beauty of life that is not affected by matters we cannot control. With the beauty of that peace in your life as you find yourself in the midst of great trials, you still have biblical peace. The peace of God provides an unending source of strength in the midst of difficulties.

In the New Testament, we see two kinds of peace; the peace which is objective and is connected to your relationship with God and the peace which is subjective and is linked to your experience in life. God alone brings peace which is not obtainable by those who are not at peace with Him.

We see an example of peace which is objective and has nothing to do with our emotional feelings in **Ephesians 6:15** *and with your feet fitted with the readiness that comes from the gospel of peace*. We also see that faith plays a role in our peace in **Romans 5:1** "*Therefore, since we have been justified through faith, we have peace with God through our Lord Jesus Christ*"

In **Philippians 4:7** "*And the peace of God, which transcends all understanding, will guard your hearts and your minds in Christ Jesus*". The peace Apostle Paul talks about is not based on worldly circumstances. It is peace that surpasses understanding. Peace which is divine and supernatural. The peace of God stands guard and keeps worry from the destroying our hearts and prevents unworthy thoughts from tearing up our minds.

As believers we know that our Lord Jesus came to bring peace. In **Isaiah 9:6-7** *6 For to us a child is born, to us a son is given, and the government will be on his shoulders. And he will be called Wonderful Counselor, Mighty God, Everlasting Father, Prince of Peace.*

7 Of the greatness of his government and peace there will be no end. He will reign on David's throne and over his kingdom, establishing and upholding it with justice and righteousness from that time on and forever. The zeal of the LORD Almighty will accomplish this.

In the above scripture, our Lord Jesus Christ is seen as the One who gives us peace. As we look again at **John 14:27** Our Lord Jesus said "My peace I give to you." This shows us how supernatural his peace is.

Our Lord Jesus Christ is seen in the two scriptures below as the dispenser of peace. We also see His beauty. He gave us His own personal peace on the cross. **Acts 10:36** *"You know the message God sent to the people of Israel, announcing the good news of peace through Jesus Christ, who is Lord of all"* and in **2 Thessalonians 3:16** *"Now may the Lord of peace himself give you peace at all times and in every way. The Lord be with all of you".*

Colossians 3:15 *Let the peace of Christ rule in your hearts, since as members of one body you were called to peace. And be thankful.* The peace of Christ is a great resource in helping us to know the will of God. As we look into this scripture, we can receive it as a plea to let the Lord's peace work in us and not as a command to seek peace. We have the peace already given to us, we must not let it rule in our hearts. We see that Apostle Paul is showing us that that peace belongs to every Christian as we are members of one body. Our peace with God and the peace of God that rules our hearts is a foundation of Christian unity.

I encourage those in my circles that there is nothing we encounter where the solution is not covered in The Bible. Personally, when I have decisions to make, I mediate on God's word and I let the peace of God direct my thoughts thereafter I examine the steps I have taken and check that there are in line with God's Word. When I have peace, I forge forward with confidence that I am aligned to God's will. As a finale, I watch God make my decisions for me.

I would encourage you all to discern that you God is present in all the decision / plans that you make. If you do not have peace and as a believer in Christ, you will feel convicted then you have probably made the wrong decision.

As we welcome the Spirit of God to rule in our lives, we open ourselves to experience His peace in us. Scripture tells us; to be spiritually minded brings life and peace, according to **Romans 8:6** *The mind governed by the flesh is death, but the mind governed by the Spirit is life and peace.*

Perfect peace comes when our focus is off the problem, off the trouble, and constantly on Christ. In **Isaiah 26:3** *You will keep in perfect peace those whose minds are steadfast, because they trust in you.*

Most people who lack peace simply have not taken the time to pursue it. God's peace comes to those with the personal discipline to stop in the midst of all things chaotic and take time to seek Him. It is a condition of peace that we cease from life's activity and know Him. He commands, *"Be still, and know that I am God"* **Psalm 46:10** And to those whose minds are steadfastly fixed on Him, He gives the gift of peace. By studying the Word of God and being taught by the Holy Spirit and permitting Him to fix our hearts on the person of Jesus Christ.

Although peace is directly related to the actions and attitudes of us individuals; we must receive it as a gift from God.

The presence of peace indicates God's blessing on our obedience. **Isaiah 48:22** tells us; *"There is no peace,"* says the LORD, *"for the wicked."* God commands us to seek peace and to make every effort to do what leads to peace" **Romans**

14:19 *Let us therefore make every effort to do what leads to peace and to mutual edification.* Naturally some people may not desire peace, but we are told in scripture that where possible, as far as it depends on us, we are to live at peace with everyone. **Romans 12:18.**

Allow God's Spirit to breathe peace into your heart and appreciate our Heavenly Father as our God of peace in line with His written word in; **1 Thessalonians 5:23.** *May God himself, the God of peace, sanctify you through and through. May your whole spirit, soul and body be kept blameless at the coming of our Lord Jesus Christ.*

May you embrace peace that allows access by one Spirit to the Father in line with; **Ephesians 2:18.** *For through him we both have access to the Father by one Spirit.*

Peace where all can be fellow-citizens with the saints **Ephesians 2:19.** Consequently, you are no longer foreigners and strangers, but fellow citizens with God's people and also members of his household.

Peace where all can be a temple in the Lord, a habitation of God in the Spirit; **Ephesians 2:20-22** *built on the foundation of the apostles and prophets, with Christ Jesus himself as the chief cornerstone* [21] *In him the whole building is joined together and rises to become a holy temple in the Lord.* [22] *And in him you too are being built together to become a dwelling in which God lives by his Spirit.*

As I come to a close on this chapter, may you always remember to keep your mind set on all the things of God in line with **Isaiah 26:3** *"You will keep in perfect peace those whose minds are steadfast, because they trust in you"* and as you remain diligent in prayer, may you always desire His peace which surpasses all understanding in line with; **Philippians 4:6-7** *Do not be anxious about anything, but in every situation, by prayer and petition, with thanksgiving, present your requests to God. And the peace* *of God, which transcends all understanding, will guard your hearts and your minds in Christ Jesus.*

Love God's word, and heed His commandments in line with **Psalm 119:165** *Great peace have those who love your law, and nothing can make them stumble* and fill your mind with spiritual thoughts in line with; **Philippians 4:8-9** *Finally, brothers and sisters, whatever is true, whatever is noble, whatever is right, whatever is pure, whatever is lovely, whatever is admirable if anything is excellent or praiseworthy think about such things. Whatever you have learned or received or heard from me, or seen in me put it into practice. And the God of peace will be with you.*

As new creation in Christ, we should always maintain peace with each other by being at peace with God first in line with His written word in **Proverbs 16:7** *When the LORD takes pleasure in anyone's way, he causes their enemies to make peace with them.*

By making peace with God, He gives us the peace within ourselves which places us in a better position to make peace with others! We must seek and pursue peace in line with **1 Peter 3:11** *They must turn from evil and do good; they must seek peace and pursue it.*

Our Lord Jesus Christ, as the Prince of peace, came to preach the message of peace to us and He died on the cross, He made peace possible with God for us.

As you go about your daily business, may you allow Our Lord Jesus to give you His peace as expressed in **2 Thessalonians 3:16** *Now may the Lord of peace himself give you peace at all times and in every way. The Lord be with all of you.*

4

PATIENCE

The FOURTH fruit is PATIENCE, what is it and what does it mean to others? Here is what my 4TH contributor had to say;

Be Joyful; Be Cheerful; Be Happy; Be Ecstatic but most of all, be PATIENT for God has something special and wonderful in his plan for you. I believe that God blessed me with a family so I could grow in patience, as I was good at exercising it outside my own household but not within and as a wife, mother and manager of a household of men of different characters, I've found myself constantly praying to God to help and give me the strength and patience to bear with them, remembering how He is patient with me always. **LUNNETTA ALE.**

A lovely reminder by my contributor that above all emotions, we should always be patient because God has something special for us. Patience is also connected to love. What does patience mean to you? Another translation is "forbearance".

My own personal experience has proven that patience is an attribute I could learn just by reading about it. I have grown to understand that it is a quality you and I can acquire by being persistent and through endurance.

The **Cambridge dictionary** says patience is: *"the ability to wait or to continue doing something despite difficulties, or to suffer without complaining or becoming annoyed"*

At the first glance of reading the Cambridge dictionary definition of patience can be quite overwhelming for someone who struggles with being patient. Exercising the ability to continue doing something despite the difficulties or to suffer without complaining can prove challenging at the best of times but it is at those precise moments that we must continue to be patient. It has also been proven true to me that the more I ask God for patience, the more apparent it seems that various trials come my way to test my patience. What I do now is ask God for His grace in dealing with whatever comes my way.

I pray that in whatever circumstances you encounter, you will find the ability within you to smile through them and receive them as opportunities to grow in patience. May you also receive those circumstances or trials of testing as our Lord Jesus training you towards His image and Him perfecting you in His love for His Glory.

The Bible as a great point of reference has many examples of those who have gone before us who demonstrated amazing levels of patience and endurance. Here are a few examples starting with three (3) examples from the **Old Testament** and two (2) from the New Testament. The first (1) example in the Old Testament comes from *"The Father of Many Nations"* Abraham. As you read through Genesis in the Bible, you see how God promised to "Abram" at that time that he would be the father of many nations **Genesis 12:1-3** Abram and his wife Sarai at that time did not have any children. As we continue to read (**Genesis chapter 13** throughout to **chapter 18**) we see that God continued to reaffirm His promise through the years However although Abram was known as a man of faith, we see in **Genesis 16** that he took his wife, Sarai's suggestion and had a child with Sarai's handmaid and Ishmael was conceived. But this was not the son God intended for Abram.

In **Genesis 17** we see Abram being renamed as Abraham and his wife Sarai as Sarah and it was at that time, God fulfilled His promise and gave them their son Isaac. From the time of God's promise to the time of His fulfilment, a number of years went by which required a lot of patience. **Hebrews 6:15** says of Abraham, *"And so, after he had patiently endured, he obtained the promise."*

And let us not be weary in well doing: for in due season we shall reap, if we faint not. **Galatians 6:9.**

Another amazing example where we see patience being demonstrated in the Bible comes from Joseph and how his brothers sold him as a slave in **Genesis 37.** As we read through scripture we see Joseph going through the 3 Ps from the pit to prison then ending up in the palace. Personally I am not sure whether I would have understood what was happening with me if I had encountered that but we see the beauty and Glory of God's work, His plan being brought to fruition in His perfect timing. When you read through the various stages of what Joseph went through, you will see how patiently and faithfully Joseph dealt with each situation, how he was led by God and how he waited for God to fulfil the promise that Joseph would be a leader of his people. Patience was key in Joseph and his family's journey for God to accomplish all that He had set us to do and for His Glory to shine forth.

Sometimes we are tested in our levels of patience because we are not patient in many instances in our life that we cry out to God and ask Him to make us patient and other times, as we are not of our own, trials / testing of patience comes from God's hand on our lives.

In the book of **Job**, we see how God's favour, he was a wealthy man and had everything great going for him and then for God's Glory and for the fulfilment of His plans we see Job lost everything through various trials which began as a result of a conversation The Lord had with Satan as referenced in; **Job 1:6-12** *"One day the angels[a] came to present themselves before the LORD, and Satan[b] also came with* *them. ⁷ The LORD said to Satan, "Where have you come from?" Satan answered the LORD, "From roaming throughout the earth, going back and forth on it.'⁸ Then the LORD said to Satan, "Have you considered my servant Job? There is no one on earth like him; he is blameless and upright, a man who fears God and shuns evil." ⁹ "Does Job fear God for nothing?" Satan replied. ¹⁰ "Have you not put a hedge around him and his household and everything he has? You have blessed the work of his hands, so that his flocks and herds are spread throughout the land.¹¹ But now stretch out your hand and strike everything he has, and he will surely curse you to your face. ¹² The LORD said to Satan, "Very well, then, everything he has is in your power, but on the man himself do not lay a finger."*

In the above scripture we can see how The Lord asked Satan who is also known as the devil, if he has considered Job and as you continue to read more of **Job 1**, you see how The Lord allowed everything Job had to be in Satan's power BUT on Job himself, Satan was not allowed to lay a finger on him.

Job lost everything he had initially been blessed with, starting with his animals (oxen, donkeys, sheep & camels etc) then his servants, then his property and more heart breaking to Job, like it would be to any of us, his sons and daughters. At the point, we read in **Job 20** *"At this, Job got up and tore his robe and shaved his head. Then he fell to the ground in worship"*

Whilst many of us would have reacted in ways which the world would champion such as losing faith in God etc, Job chose to worship and not curse God for he understood and accepted that, what The Lord gave him, The Lord took away. Further down in scripture we see how despite how Job's friends tried to be there for him and despite what advice or thoughts they gave to him, Job trusted in God's ways. This took a lot of patience and trust in God's plans and as a result of endurance, in **Job 42:10** we see how God restored to Job twice as much as he had in the former years.

As we move into the **New Testament**, one (1) example of patience and endurance comes from Simeon and the patience he demonstrated as he waited for the Messiah.

In **Luke 2:25,** we read the following; *25 Now there was a man in Jerusalem called Simeon, who was righteous and devout. He was waiting for the consolation of Israel, and the Holy Spirit was on him. 26 It had been revealed to him by the Holy Spirit that he would not die before he had seen the Lord's Messiah.*

From verse **Luke 2:27** we read how Simeon was moved by the Spirit, he went into the temple courts, shortly after Mary and Joseph took baby Jesus to the temple to give an offering to God for the birth of their child.

We read from the Bible that The Holy Ghost had revealed to Simeon that he would not see death until he had seen the birth of The Messiah. We know from the word that Simeon would not die until he saw the Saviour, which in itself indicates he endured a long waiting period. When Joseph and Mary took The baby Jesus into the temple, Simeon was led by the Spirit to visit Him there and as soon as he saw Him. Simeon took Jesus in his arms and thanked God that the promised child had arrived. Simeon knew that he could depart in peace.

The 2nd example in the New Testament comes from our Lord and Saviour, Jesus Christ where he demonstrated an example of Patience none of us can even measure up to at any level.

In **Hebrews 12** we read that whilst our Lord Jesus was on the cross He endured opposition from sinners but yet His crucifixion was for our salvation. Before Jesus arrived at the cross He patiently trained the disciples. Even after His miracles and proclamations of being the Son of God, the disciples were often confused as to who Jesus was. Today we think of the disciples as being mature men of faith. But as we read through the gospel accounts, Jesus was still trying to teach them how to persevere in prayer up until the moment He was taken in the garden to be crucified.

As a point of reflection, I hope whatever task God has called us to fulfil, we need to continue doing the work even if we do not see the progress we would like to see and I pray that we will continue to serve The Lord with patience.. Despite knowing His death was approaching, our Lord Jesus continued to teach His disciples until the moment of His death. As I mentioned earlier, our Lord Jesus demonstrated a level of patience we cannot measure nor can we even compare ourselves to. With that understanding, I hope you will continue to rejoice and delight in Him for greater is our God who resides in us than he who is of this world.

5

KINDNESS

The FIFTH fruit is KINDNESS, what is it and what does it mean to others? Here is what my 5TH contributor had to say;

Every born again Christian who has believed and confessed Jesus Christ as their Lord and saviour (Romans 10v 9-10), has the capacity to produce the fruits of the spirit, as they have already been given to those who are born again, deposited in their spirit, one of, which is Kindness. It becomes your responsibility to grow that fruit of kindness that God has given you into a mighty tree, which gives you a great harvest of fruits expressing and manifesting the Kindness of Christ who lives in you.

To walk in kindness, is a choice and therefore as children of God, it must become our deliberate attempt to walk in kindness all the time, against all odds. Our Lord Jesus was compassionate, kind, gentle, manifesting the fruit and a great harvest of Kindness.

To manifest kindness we have to sow the right seeds into our heart, our spirit. (even as faith comes by hearing and hearing the word of God) so does our human spirit respond to what we hear, and the seeds that have been sown in our heart. **HELEN NANJIRA GREGORY.**

Another great contribution above and a great reminder that as a believer of our Lord and Saviour Jesus Christ, we have the capacity to produce the fruit of Kindness, therefore we have a responsibility to grow that fruit.

Ok, first things first, when I reflect on what Kindness is / could be, the following definitions come to memory; being mindful of others, being considerate, putting others before self, being sweet and being full of warmth etc

Two questions to ponder, (1) how can you and I grow the fruit of kindness generally? And (2) how can we grow the fruit of kindness in the different areas of our lives such as in work, church, social circles etc., on a daily basis?

After some quiet time and meditation, the one key answer, which comes to mind regarding how we can grow in the fruit of Kindness and any other through fruit is through The Indwelling Holy Spirit. Like with any of the other 8 fruits, growing the fruit of Kindness has to be done in partnership with The Holy Spirit, otherwise our attempts will result in birthing something else from the flesh.

Growth in the fruit of Kindness is not automatic. Although our Heavenly Father has given us the ability and the freedom to choose or as many have claimed "freewill" etc., as Christians, personally for me, choosing to partner with the Holy Spirit is the best decision I have ever made. That decision has made my growth in all fruits of the Spirit enjoyable and light, which is great as the Word teaches us to release any heaviness / burdens, our York is thus light. As we look to our Heavenly Father and as we abide with our Lord Jesus Christ and as we allow the Holy Spirit to lead us in ALL things, the path in which we take will be paved out for us, there is beauty in allowing our steps to be ordered. May I encourage you to seek and allow The Holy Spirit in every step of your growth?

In my personal walk with God, I have grown to witness the following qualities within myself; not allowing my peace to be disturbed in any circumstances, being well maintained and just trusting that it is well with my soul, that The Great I am who resides in me, has got me covered.

Through the written Word, we know that our Lord Jesus is the perfect example of someone who operates in the fruit of

Kindness and all other fruits. In **Psalm 23:2-3,** we see that that through the fruit of Kindness, our Heavenly Father gives us green pastures, quiet waters and the restoration of our souls when we are feeling tired / burdened.

Another example in the Bible of our Heavenly Father's expression of Kindness is in the book of Kings where we read about Prophet Elijah and the widow woman in Zarephath when there was a drought in the land. As we read more in the same book of Kings, we also see another instance where our Heavenly Father showed more kindness when He raised the widow's only son from the dead **1 Kings 17:8-24.**

There are many examples we can all read, soak in and meditate on such as in **Genesis 21:9-21** when Sarah asked Hagar and Ishmael to leave after seeing the implications of the earlier decision she made as referenced earlier in the chapter of Patience. Our Heavenly Father showed kindness to Hagar and Ishmael in the form of water and hope in kindness He "gathers the lambs in his arms and carries them close to his heart; he gently leads those that have young" **Isaiah 40:11**.

Where there is Kindness, sinners are rescued and souls are saved, additionally, cleansing and renewal takes place through the workings of The Holy Spirit. **Titus 3: 3-6** sums up the condition of humanity "*For we ourselves were also once foolish, disobedient, deceived, serving various lusts and pleasures, living in malice and envy, hateful and hating one another. But when the kindness and the love of God our Saviour toward man appeared, not by works of righteousness which we have done, but according to His mercy He saved us, through the washing of regeneration and renewing of the Holy Spirit, whom He poured out on us abundantly through Jesus Christ our Saviour.*"

Kindness is shown in acts of compassion and generosity, in spite of ingratitude. The parable of The Good Samaritan is

another great example where we read about a man who was beaten up, robbed and left to die. We read how both a priest and a Levite passed by the suffering man, but finally a Samaritan stopped. "*And when he saw him, he had compassion. So he went to him and bandaged his wounds, pouring on oil and wine; and he set him on his own animal, brought him to an inn, and took care of him. On the next day, when he departed, he took out two denarii, gave them to the innkeeper, and said to him, 'Take care of him; and whatever more you spend, when I come again, I will repay you.'*"
Luke 10:33-35.

Showing kindness to people should not really be an act we follow / do which requires a formula. When we show the kindness of God, our approach becomes tender and beneficial to others. As we grow in the fruit of kindness, we should find that every action we take, together with every spoken word, God's grace is present. To maintain this attitude toward those we love is hard enough, to show kindness toward those who are against us requires the work of God **2 Corinthians 6:4-6**.

To conclude, I honestly believe and I can testify that as I have allowed The Holy Spirit to work in me and with me and through me, the fruit of kindness has manifested itself beautifully. In my attempt to reach out to others and to place their needs before my own, I have enhanced my calmness levels. I have also grown to resist the deception of the flesh. For many, this is an area people get deceived as they convince themselves that it was really their decision when they follow the leading of their human desires, which is where the deception of flesh comes in.

My prayer and hope for us all is that as we witness the growth and see the manifestation of the fruit of Kindness, we will be able to remain calm and we will not allow issues / situations beyond our control to push our buttons as so to speak, which would normally be the case when the fruit of Kindness is not in operation. A reminder of how you can check whether the fruit of Kindness is in operation in your life is through your desire in meeting the needs of others and also your drive serving others in Kindness.

As a believer in Christ, one way you can assess where you are in the growth of the fruit of Kindness operating in you, the fruit of Kindness should heighten your level of encouragement in others, it should improve your interaction and how you fellowship with those around you. As you live and grow in Kindness, others will be attracted to the same fruit of Kindness, which resides in the inner you.

6

GOODNESS

The SIXTH fruit is GOODNESS, what is it and what does it mean to others? Here is what my 6TH contributor had to say;

What Goodness means to me. For me Goodness means doing something that pleases God and something that other people can be thankful for. Giving to the poor/needy, caring for one another, visiting the sick, and volunteering in the community are my examples of Goodness. Doing these things is good for me and those around me. Most importantly God wants me to show his Goodness based on his commandments and his character. **SARAH HOMBARUME.**

I share the sentiments in the above contribution in connecting Goodness to pleasing God and through the fruit of Goodness, being of service to others in our giving and caring, an act which symbolises the Love of our Lord.
Goodness is having a quality of being good. As a fruit of The Spirit, Goodness is being honest, honourable, compassionate and generous.

Another representation of goodness takes our virtue and excellence and models it to others in the action of love. It is doing the right thing even when it does not feel like we should, as Joseph was betrayed and sold as a slave, he chose to make his situation good and help and treat others better than he needed too. Goodness is the model for people to repent and accept Christ.

Let us look at what scripture says; in **Ephesians 5:9;** *for the fruit of the Spirit is in all goodness and righteousness and truth."* And in **2 Thessalonians 1:11;** *"Wherefore also we pray always for you, that our God would count you worthy of this calling, and fulfil all the good pleasure of his goodness, and the work of faith with power."*

How can the fruit of goodness be measured in us? By you and I choosing to see the good in others before they see it themselves. As we live and aim to grow in the fruit of goodness, let us be mindful that our conduct / approach is not just a matter of us doing good things or being taught what is good.

Seeking more of the fruit of goodness in our conduct, leads us into doing what is good and in doing what is good enables us to grasp the real teaching of what our Heavenly Father desires us to do. Goodness as a fruit of the Spirit should be reflected our attitude as a child of God. We should see the manifestation as it flows forth from the Holy Spirit.

Personally I have grown to understand that the very root of all goodness is from God and I believe, as we live and grow in the fruit of goodness, we should be able to see the blessings which comes all the fruits of The Holy Spirit. I pray that as we go through various circumstances, be it, the good, the bad and the not so pleasant, we will be humble enough to not only know but to acknowledge that God is always there for us.

The fruit of goodness is defined by God's love and by His light. May we love like He first loved us and May we seek His light everywhere we go and in everything we do, when we do that, seeing goodness in others will become easy for us.

Romans 7:21 tells us while we are actually doing well, we know that it is not our goodness, but the fruit of goodness that is in us. When we live and grow in the fruit of goodness, we are able to overcome our nature to do that which is evil.

Like in **Psalm 23** where, David (the man after God's own heart) proclaimed: "Surely goodness and mercy shall follow me all the days of my life", we too must declare and repeat the same as pursue all things which are good and truly representative of what our Heavenly Father stands for.

We see all throughout scripture that goodness like every fruit of The Spirit is all part of our Heavenly Father's nature. In the "goodness" of God, we see His Grace and His abundant generosity in providing for all of our daily needs.

We live in a world where many terms compliment one another, like, husband and wife etc. **Ephesians 5:9** states "His goodness is closely associated with *righteousness* and *truth.*" What does Righteousness and Truth mean for you and I? As we are looking at what the fruit of goodness is, one of the scriptures of righteousness I feel helps to answer this question is **Psalms 106:3** which says; *"Blessed are they who observe justice, who do righteousness at all times!"* So, we can see that being righteous goes hand in hand with observing justice and as we do that, we are blessed, which from observation, I feel is more evident if you become flexible enough to allow goodness to work in you.

And as we look at what Truth should mean for us, In **Psalms 145:18** we are encouraged to call onto our Lord in truth and as we do so, He is near to all who call on him. Not sure about you, but with that revelation, would you not want to live in truth knowing that as you do so, you are near to The Lord.

May we continue to be encouraged to bear much fruit and as we do that on a daily basis, may we be open to receive God's goodness and enlarge our capacity. Let us live our lives through the example of our Lord of Lords and King of Kings, our Lord Jesus and keep doing that which is good in line with His written word in **Acts 10:38**.

In all things, even in situations where people are against you, may you be further encouraged in line with **Luke 6:27-2** and *do good to everyone,* even our *enemies".* We are told to not only love our enemies, but to do well to those who hate us and to bless those who curse us, and to pray for those who spitefully use us. May God be Glorified, in Jesus's name, Amen.

As I conclude on this chapter, join me in asking yourself a few questions; is the fruit of goodness operating in me and if not yet, what can I do about it? As I gear up to thoroughly answer that question for myself, let us all be reminded of **Galatians 6:9**, "And let us not grow weary of doing **good**, for in due season we will reap, if we do not give up."

Another great and effective way to measure the growth of your goodness is by monitoring yourself daily both in conduct and your attitude in various scenarios (the pleasant ones and in those situations you cannot control) and constructively but truthfully assessing yourself on how good you have been.

Measuring the growth is great and even more crucial is to be in a place of awareness when the things which you do daily believing you are doing no harm to anyone are not actually indirectly blocking the growth of goodness in you. Here are a few examples of how you could be blocking the flow of growth;

When you support a friend's ungodly behavior (for the sake of your loyalty to them), knowing that what they are doing is wrong but because it is not you taking that action directly, you believe you are doing well. From another perspective, when you commit a sin, which comes easily to many of us, whether on a smaller / bigger scale but instead of taking ownership and repent, you claim you were led by the Spirit.

Let the goodness of our Heavenly Father endure continually. Let us be open to a long term commitment to doing good and that which is right

7

FAITHFULNESS

The SEVENTH fruit is FAITHFULNESS, what is it and what does it mean to others? Here is what my 7TH contributor had to say;

Faithfulness is a harmony between what I believe in and what I do, considered on three different levels:

1. Faithfulness to God – If I obey God's commandments point 2 and 3 will be easy to maintain.

2. Faithfulness to myself – I stand for what I think is right.

3. Faithfulness to my husband – Not only being seen as avoiding a desire for someone else, but being my husband's pride and support, even if I may disagree with some of his opinions. **KASIA ZARCZYNSKA.**

My contributor above brings a different perspective to what faithfulness means to her, not only from a personal note but from the level which places God first. For many of us, we too can relate as most of us see faithfulness being centered around what we place a high value on and faithfulness being placed on what we see as important such as the commitment in our families, work etc.

In my personal view, faithfulness represents that which is persistent / constant in one's life and that which valued highly such as in a marriage, and standing on the vows which were made regardless of what hardship may come. I pray that in all areas of your life, you remain / choose to be dedicated and devoted to the decisions you make today, tomorrow and always. From a biblical perspective, when I was reflecting on this fruit and what it means from a deeper level, my thoughts went to **2 Corinthians 5:7** *For we walk by faith, not by sight.*

What does faithfulness mean to you and how do you justify being faithful? Like in my early chapters, let us first look at what faithfulness means in the eyes of God, our Father and our Creator in Heaven.

The best example of faithfulness, like with all the other fruits is our Heavenly Father. For those who like to copy what others are doing, such as someone they are inspired by, in building up our characters, may I encourage you as I am encouraging myself in the same light, to copy the example of our Heavenly Father in His representation of Faithfulness. Our Heavenly Father is faithful in fulfilling His role in the growth and shaping of our character. That which He starts, He brings to completion in His perfect time.

When you take being faithful at its basic definition and when you look at it from the various definitions in a dictionary, you will come across the following characteristic traits; being honest or being loyal etc. Many people to cover up their shortcomings when they fail to be faithful in which context, say it was through a weak moment or that they were tempted etc. When you are connected to the true vine and decide that you are not of your own and you cry out and say, God, cleanse me, purify me and refine me, take everything out of me, which is not of you, you will start to understand the following scripture from a deeper place **1 Corinthians 10:13** *"Do not say you were tempted / that you were weak" The temptations* *in your life are no different from what others experience. And God is faithful. He will not allow the temptation to be more than you can stand. When you are tempted, he will show you a way out so that you can endure"*

What I have grown to understand and to appreciate on a higher level is that, scripture tells us that our Heavenly Father never gives us trials we cannot handle. His faithfulness gives us great assurance that all the trials we face / encounter will be in proportion to our strength.

Most people say it is not easy to be faithful as we live in an imperfect world, which is full of our own personal agendas. I pray both you and I's spiritual eyes are open to the worldly deception so that indirectly, we do not end up contributing to an environment, which daily makes it difficult to remain faithful in the circles we allow ourselves to be in and in the conversations we allow others to draw us in and keep us engages in be in in our work / private gatherings / even in the church!

Let us be mindful and make it our personal target to say no to the things of this world, which always seem appealing to the moral and ethical standards lower than those offered to us by our Heavenly Father, The Great I AM and let us hunger for His way of life.

May we not accept as normal that which is evidently wrong, such as lying, stealing or coveting and indirectly end up promoting such acts within our culture. Saying nothing when you see such acts and doing nothing is actually you doing something, you indirectly support that which you see as wrong but still choose to give a blind eye to it.

Do you recognise when you cease being faithful? One indicator is when you see and accept the destruction around as normal to you, therefore you accept it and again, you keep a blind eye to things you should perhaps be stepping forward and doing something about them. More than ever we see cases of people breaking agreements, taking promises lightly, which they once made strongly. We see in the media / around us the mis-description of products / manufacturers telling sugar coated truth regarding the quality of the products. We see people breaking / bending rules to suit their own agendas or to suit those they personally favour, again, forgetting that we serve an all seeing God, one who is fair and justice and one whose plans will prevail regardless of what man's agenda is.

As I read through scripture, I note one example of unfaithfulness where Prophet Jeremiah's heart was torn apart by the unfaithfulness of God's people with particular reference to the point when the nation had forgotten God's law and made idols for themselves and as a result of that, he foresaw God's judgement.

Many are still claiming events of what transpired in the old testament in terms of how life was lived in order to justify how they are living now and the type of lifestyle they choose to still maintain, one which commits them to sin, despite the many convictions they may have daily pressing them to choose the narrow way, forgetting there is a new testament, which serves as a revelation showing us the timeline from, when our Lord Jesus was born to His second coming. We should pay more attention to the revelation of the New Testament, which makes clear to us that our Lord Jesus and Savior, lived, died and arose so that us believers, who receive Him as Christ might have eternal life.

Am I saying we should forget the Old Testament? No, why, because besides any of us not having the authority to say so, our Lord Jesus made it clear, he came to fulfil the old testament, it is written in **Matthew 5:17;** "*Do not think that I have come to abolish the Law or the Prophets; I have not come to abolish them but to fulfil them*"

I pray that in our quest to grow the fruit of faithfulness, alongside the other 8 fruit(s), we will be more alert and open to receive the New Testament as our guide on how to worship God today.

I read the following statement from **http://www.bible.ca/** which fits in perfectly in terms of how we should receive the Old and the New Testament; "*the Old is the New concealed and the New is the Old revealed. The Old Testament was preparatory, temporary, and limited. The New is complete, eternal, and universal. The Old Testament promised a New Testament (Jer. 31:31). The prophet Isaiah spoke of the days to come when the new law would go forth from Jerusalem (Isaiah 2:2-4). In the New Testament, the Apostle Paul stated that the law of Moses had been given until the seed, which is Christ Jesus, had come (study Galatians 3:19-27)*"

One of my favourite saying is "today, have a serious word with yourself" and I will say it here again, additionally, I would like to challenge you to truly ask yourself an honest question, where are you in growing the fruit of faithfulness?. As Faithlessness continues to rise to higher levels in all areas of society due to the many selfish ways and as many continue to be drawn to all the worldly things which provide temporary pleasure / victories and therefore directly / indirectly, they resist the good and salty things which our Heavenly Father has offered us in His word, may I please encourage you to seek the higher truth.

I have been part of several debates where people say "but, we are free to choose as we will" When it comes to the subject of freewill, many choose definitions which suit their current situations, again forgetting we serve an all seeing God whose word makes it clear that many are the plans in man's heart but nevertheless, God's plans will prevail. I personally feel, in my "freewill", choosing to be aligned with God's will and choosing to place God at the core centre in my life is the best choice I could possibly ever make, furthermore I feel, it is the best option in order for us to not only grow in our faithfulness but also to enhance our growth rate on a frequent basis.

Let us draw near to our Lord and Saviour, whose faithfulness is part of His grace and whose faithfulness means that His character is consistent. His word tells us in **Hebrews 13:8** that *Jesus Christ is the same yesterday and today and forever.*

Since God is faithful, let us accept our responsibility to imitate Him in being faithful by committing our lives to well doing and let us be encouraged by another example in the Old Testament of Ruth's extraordinary faithfulness, who chose in her "freewill" to maintain her loyalty to Naomi and the great sacrifices she made to go with Naomi to what was a foreign land to her. We see how God moved in her life through the unusual blessings Boaz, as a godly man gave her as a result of her faithfulness to Naomi. Where there is faithfulness, regardless of hardship / circumstances beyond our control, God's hand is evident and His is faithful to His promises.

8

GENTLENESS

The EIGTH fruit is GENTLENESS, what is it and what does it mean to others? Here is what my 8TH contributor had to say;

What is Gentleness? Gentleness is the 8th attribute of the Spirit (Galatians 5:23) Gentleness refers to action, whereas meekness refers to attitude. Gentleness evidences itself in a willingness to yield result. I believe gentleness encompasses humility, politeness towards others. It does not mean weakness; it involves restrained behavior towards others. The opposite of gentleness is anger and arrogance; an attribute that does not encourage the Spirit to nurture and grow.

I have often witnessed soft or gentle words or reaction turning anger around and allowing willingness to yield. This rings true to me, as a teenager I tended to show willingness (yield result) when reprimanded for wrong doing when spoken to with gentleness but firm manner. The opposite is true, often harsh words stir up anger and hatred. I believe a whisper can be louder than a scream. I believe anyone can be gentle, if one yields oneself to Jesus' offer of His Gentleness as a gift. We can be filled with the fruit of gentleness if we allow The Holy Spirit to lead us in all we do.

Blessed are the meek for they shall inherit the kingdom of God (Matthew 5:5) Who wouldn't want to be part of the blessed gift, I ask?
PATRICIA NALISHUWA.

Great contribution above and one which has the potential to start off many other conversations based on some of the key attributes such as "Gentleness does not mean weakness" and this is where I wanted to come in and add my add my thoughts. Another definition of Gentleness is Meekness, therefore I agree that meekness does not translate weakness! Which unfortunately many people believe to be the case.

We also see in scripture where gentleness is referenced as meekness. In **2 Corinthians 10:1** *"Now I, Paul, myself am pleading with you by the meekness and gentleness of Christ—who in presence am lowly among you, but being absent am bold toward you."*

Meekness and *lowly* in conjunction with gentleness. These words help show that gentleness requires humility, because along with pride and feelings of superiority come rough reactions and stubborn, know-it-all answers.

We hear the word **gentle** spoken very loosely in other contexts such as "gentleman" in scenarios where polite men as an example, open doors or pull up chairs for their mothers / wives etc. In other examples, we hear the word **gentle / see it in action** in the context of a parent to child relationship, such as in the case of new fathers, some of whom I have watched pick up their new born with much care and softness from the fear that should they enforce their normal strength, they may harm the child. I have witnessed one of the new fathers in my church seek (the child's Grandmother) his mother's assistance in holding / lifting up his newborn because he, out of much love and a strong desire to be "gentle" is scared he may harm the baby should he be the one to lift his baby because he recognises he is of a particular strength. I have seen on several occasions where those we see as the strongest of them all melt and become "gentle" at the sight of a new born.

Let us look at our Lord of Lords and King of Kings' example of gentleness. In **Matthew 11:29**, Christ said, *"Take My yoke upon you and learn from Me, for I am gentle and lowly in heart, and you will find rest for your souls"*

What does gentleness personally mean to you? Some research has demonstrated that gentleness is linked to having a humble and meek attitude and having the desire to help others instead of wanting to be superior to them. I hope you will start to see within yourself that as attitude like that flows from a spirit of showing real love for others and having a real interest in their well-being and that, which concerns them.

Drawing us back into scripture, **Philippians 4:5** tells us to *"let your gentleness be known to all men. The Lord is at hand."* The written word is very clear. We can see that our Heavenly Father encourages us to be gentle in our thoughts and in our actions. When we really reflect on who God is, the Alpha and Omega, the Beginning and the End, not sure about you but I personally cannot end begin to claim that my mind can measure ALL the power He possess in the universe, His universe, the one He created but yet for those who walk closely with Him and for those who hunger for His ways daily, we can see how gentle He is with us. I strongly encourage you to place Him as your example and choose to not only learn to be like Him but pay attention to His written word and heed His every instruction.

Another key connection in this fruit is **humility**, which we are shown as being closely connected with gentleness. Both **James 4:6** and **1 Peter 5:5** teaches us that *"God resists the proud, but gives grace to the humble"* What I have taken from that particular word is that, as God resists the pride, we are not to be limited to those we are gentle with, we must work hard and still be gentle to everyone, even to those who have upset us, those who have caused us an offence, overall, those who in our natural perspective do not feel deserve gentleness.

Let us continue to be encouraged by examples of our Lord Jesus Christ's gentleness, such as that He showed us in **John 8:1-11** where many wanted to stone the woman who was caught in adultery. When many were ready to cast that first stone at a sinner, our Lord Jesus taught us to follow His example by gently telling those we see as "sinners" when we all are, to go and sin no more. That example alone demonstrated a great example of gentleness, which our Heavenly Father wants us all to learn from.

In our cry out for our loved ones to be saved, let us desire more and more of every fruit of the Spirit. Let us demonstrate gentleness in all that we do and in turn, let us help our loved ones and friends and their friends truly change their ways of being and come to accept our Heavenly Father through seeing our gentle approach towards them.

In your daily quest to be gentle, here are some of the questions you can ask yourself in your work / at home;

1. Was I as gentle in that dialogue as our Heavenly Father has shown me to be?

2. In my mission to lead many to Christ, is my approach gentle to communicate the message of not being in sin or do I present myself in a holier than thou mode?

Let us continue to be reminded that gentleness does not mean weakness and instead, let us receive gentleness in addition to the other 8 fruit(s) as God's Holy Spirit being active in our lives. In this time and age, many people struggle or simply choose to not exhibit gentleness in a world where through the deception of the enemy, they are lost in darkness hence being content amongst those who are cruel and those who cause deliberate harm to others. It is written that our

God disciplines those He Loves. He shows us what we would receive as tough love but because He is God, He carries the mark of gentleness.

Let me share with you the beauty I have personally encountered from seeking and growing daily the fruits of The Holy Spirit and in this case, the fruit of gentleness; when I am in a conversation and I know with facts that what someone else is coming back to me with is off key, I am able to offer a different perspective with ease instead of throwing a tantrum or storming off in anger, which would only affect me longer term. I forgive quickly and easily, otherwise what good is there in me carrying all that un-forgiveness comes with. In all my dialogues, salvation for others is my key driving force and I owe that to The Holy Spirit, because of The Holy Spirit, without it, I would probably be sharing this in a different context.

As I come to a close on this chapter, visualise the beautiful and wonderful display of gentleness our Lord Jesus showed us in **Matthew 21:5** when He, our King of Kings came to us, gentle whilst riding on a donkey. Allow The Holy Spirit by inviting Him into your presence, to lead you and be filled with the fruit of gentleness on a level you could never reach from your own efforts. Be open to receive and for others to see a powerful gentleness sealed with the mark of our most High and forever faithful God.

9

SELF CONTROL

The NINTH fruit is SELF-CONTROL, what is it and what does it mean to others? Here is what my 9TH contributor had to say;

> *There are two parts in the book of Matthew that come to mind when I think about self-control. The first concerns the parable of the mustard seed. It has taught me that if I possess even the smallest amount of belief and cultivate it, it can grow into a tree whose branches will extend and be rooted in faith. I sometimes feel that though I have faith in Him, I may not always trust in Him. When I lack patience and grow anxious I do not always allow Him to show me the way. My only comfort becomes prayer and His word and then I am reminded that faith does move mountains if I choose to trust in His plan over my own. It requires consistency and faith but none are possible without self-control.*
>
> *The second is that of Matthew 22:37. It tells us to "Love the Lord your God with all your heart & with all your soul & with all your mind. This is the first and greatest commandment". There is so much peace in this for myself because it's like no matter what, it all starts with me. It requires self-control and it is a choice: to seek Him first with my heart, soul and mind. The journey continues.* **SUZANNE CHILESHE.**

We now come to the last fruit of the Holy Spirit, Glory to God for His favour. Thank you to my contributor above who has given us her perspective of Self Control in two personal settings backed up with scripture reference and the following statement declared, "it starts with me" I agree with that. In everything we choose to do, it really starts with us. If we choose the wide gate which leads to many distractions, that decision started with us, in our personal choices. I pray you choose the narrow road and heed God's instructions and bring your will into alignment with His perfect will for you.

When The Holy Spirit is active and operational in us, the changes you begin to see in yourself and in fellow believers are due to The Holy Spirit's work in us. Although saying yes to God's will and desiring everything He offers us starts with us, we do not become a Christian from our own abilities, nor do we grow through our own strength as much as many through deception claim "they made something happen through their own sole efforts". It is written in **Philippians 2:13** that *"it is God who is at work in you, both to will and to work for His good pleasure."* I say a jubilant Amen to that scripture.

Self-control as you and I may know is the ability to control ourselves in many scenarios such as when someone disregards us / goes ahead of us in a queue when we have been standing for a long time etc.. When the fruit of Self-control is evident in us, we take things in moderation and the ability to say "no" when we need to do so and especially when many are faced with peer pressure.

Here is another definition of Self-control taken from **Wikipedia** as the many people' "go to" source for information; Self-control is *"the ability to control one's emotions, behavior, and desires in the face of external demands, to function in society"*.

When you desire to grow in your walk with God and when you say, like I do more times than not, "Holy Spirit you are always welcome in my midst and as you allow Him to do as He wills", one evidence of His presence and the work of Self-control as a fruit of The Holy Spirit, is your ability to control your own thoughts and that which you choose to do in line with God's ways. Without the Holy Spirit active in us, we operate in the flesh, where our fallen nature is controlled by sin, where danger is stronger and the ability to choose wisely and correctly is lost.

We know from scripture that we are in this world but we are

not of this world. As believers, more than ever, we need the fruit of self-control fully active because it is written in **Romans 7:21-25**; *"21 I have discovered this principle of life—that when I want to do what is right, I inevitably do what is wrong. 22 I love God's law with all my heart.23 But there is another power[a] within me that is at war with my mind. This power makes me a slave to the sin that is still within me. 24 Oh, what a miserable person I am! Who will free me from this life that is dominated by sin and death? 25 Thank God! The answer is in Jesus Christ our Lord. So you see how it is: In my mind I really want to obey God's law, but because of my sinful nature I am a slave to sin".*

Just from the first verse of that scripture we must be armed with self-control as we see already that not only do we deal with external matters but we also fight with internal forces. We also know in the written word in the book of Ephesians that we do not wrestle against the flesh but against principalities of the world. Read my FIRST Book; Embracing Number 7 for more insight into that scripture.

Self-control goes hand in hand with perseverance; **2 Peter 1:5-6**; *"5 For this very reason, make every effort to add to your faith goodness; and to goodness, knowledge; 6 and to knowledge, self-control; and to self-control, perseverance; and to perseverance, godliness"*

Embrace everything the fruit of The Holy Spirit brings into your life. As I am focusing on Self-control in this particular chapter, take joy in the knowledge that it diminishes our fleshly desires to indulge in the foolish things of the world, those things which convinces us in our minds that they feel good or that we are the ones who actually want them. When you look at the word "Self-control" it can easily translate an ability for you to control things within your control through your own strength. As a born-again Christian, your heart is made new, you are transformed and what used to make perfect sense to you in the natural ceases to do so. Rejoice as a new creation in Christ, having Self-control for you translates, having "control over your own behaviour and taking your mind and emotions captive both internally and externally through the power of our living God, not through your own strength. Let our Father in Heaven receive ALL the Glory.

Through your heart and through being watchful of what you allow to not only enter but dominate your mind, you can begin to determine / establish where you are through the work of the fruit of The Holy Spirit in your life.

We read in scripture" Self-control being spoken of in areas of our bodies, which as a believer I accept to be a vessel for The Holy Spirit's indwelling. In **1 Thessalonians 4:3–5**, we are told; *"³ God's will is for you to be holy, so stay away from all sexual sin. ⁴ Then each of you will control his own body[a] and live in holiness and honor— ⁵ not in lustful passion like the pagans who do not know God and his ways".* With that in mind, mediate on it and keep your body under control.

When we seek out Self-control and receive it with an open heart, from above and allow it to be worked out in us through The Holy Spirit, there is timeless beauty in it. With all things, do not seek it through your own works / from worldly activities and therefore have self-praise, instead, seek it from our Father in Heaven and praise Him for it, He alone deserves ALL the Glory. Let us not adopt an attitude of "I have accepted Christ, therefore the fruit(s) of The Holy Spirit is active in me" Do not be that passive, receive God's gift and be active in its operation. Our Heavenly Father is the source but with us saying "Yes Father, in Jesus's name, Holy Spirit come in and take charge" we partner up with our Father in Heaven. I came across this quote and I agree with it; *"We are promised the gift of self-control, yet we also must take it by force."*

I want to encourage you all to pull away from self-praise and from temporary victories especially if you stand as a true believer in Christ. I personally say, let our Lord of Lords, our King of Kings, Jesus Christ get ALL the Glory. Let your self-control come from the power He supplies.

When we allow the love of Christ to control us and when we embrace the truth that He is our beginning and our ending, we can bask in the liberty that we need not muster our own strength to exercise self-control, but we can find in our Lord and saviour, Jesus Christ. Let us embrace the self-control, which comes under the control of our Lord Jesus Christ through the power of His Spirit.

As a fellow believer, as you receive self-control as a fruit produced in and through you by God's Spirit, The Holy Spirit, may you take courage in the growth rate of this fruit in addition to other 8 fruit(s) mentioned above in earlier chapters.

Here are some indicators of how you can measure / see the evidence of Self-control in your life;

Emotions / actions; are they in charge of you? Or have you mastered them? It is written in **Proverbs 25:28** *"A person without self-control is like a city with broken-down walls."*

That which you speak; Is your mind protected as it serves as a gateway to your soul, are you aware and in control of that which you speak and not what has been sown into you? It is written in **Proverbs 13:3** *"Be careful what you say and protect your life. A careless talker destroys himself."*

It is also written, life and death are in the tip of your tongue, additionally I say, what you speak, and you give life to. As I bring this chapter to an end and as I prepare to go into further reflections, I pray that your hunger for self- control bypasses your self-definition and you grab hold of that which our Heavenly Father offers us through His Holy Spirit in Jesus's name. Rejoice and call on God, speak His written word, He watches over it and it never returns void.

10

FURTHER REFLECTIONS

There you have it. The definitions and my personal notes / additions within the various chapters or through my contributors' collective understand of The Holy Spirit is not limited to what has been covered in this book. It is written in the book of Isaiah (I will not give the chapter / verse so that in your hunger, you can search it out) Our thoughts are not like our Heavenly Father's thoughts and neither are His ways like ours so there is no way can this book cover everything nor was it my personal attempt to do so. I am grateful for that which our Heavenly Father has allowed me to put together in this book through the STAR of this book, His Holy Spirit and through my Lord of Lords interceding for me, for the completion of this book.

It's easy to see how the attributes among the fruit of the Spirit overlap and relate to each other. Meekness and gentleness relate very closely to love, longsuffering (being patient and not short-tempered), kindness and self-control.
We surely need meekness and gentleness in place of "hatred, contentions, and jealousies, outbursts of wrath, selfish ambitions, and dissensions"!

Some of the key elements and conversations I picked up on when I gave a fruit of The Holy Spirit to each of my 9 contributors was that it was tricky to separate them and I agree, they are all interlinked but they do produce distinctive results.

Reflecting on some of the fruit(s) mentioned above, remember that whilst Gentleness includes true humility, it does not mean we you and I hunger for it, we are not to see ourselves as being far too important or above a certain role to take on certain tasks.

Also, be reminded that as mentioned above, gentleness does not translate weakness, may you instead receive it like all other 8 fruit(s) as being a part of God's character, the one who moves in victory, the greater one who resides in you.

In **Numbers 12:3**, we read how Moses in his high position given to him by our God, was so humble, he excelled in meekness. In your quest to bask in the fruit(s) of The Holy Spirit, let everything be about God's agenda and not your own.

Be encouraged and rejoice for the 9 fruit(s) of The Holy Spirit come directly from God, our Father in Heaven Himself. Through ordered steps, I have been led to particular people of God, fellow brothers and sisters in Christ whom I have learnt priceless lessons from, for which I am truly thankful. One lesson I learnt from Pastor Benny Hinn and Prophet Brian Carn is that The Holy Spirit is a gentleman, who does not force Himself on any of us, we must therefore invite Him into our midst. I am saying to you and everyone else to prioritise working daily with The Holy Spirit in fusing in ALL 9 fruit (s) in your life and everything about you. I pray as you read more and seek more of God's word and how His Holy Spirit works in you, you will experience a dramatic shift and see changes in the quality of your life and well-being.

Every fruit on reflection represents such a powerful ability to change, transform, and sanctify you and in turn, create a shift in your environment and in those around you, who will see the Glory of our Lord evident in your life, shining in every area of you.

I mention this in **Embracing Number 7**, personally, as I walk and operate in the 9 fruit (s) I can testify that without saying anything, non-believers in addition to believers have been drawn to me because in some of their own words, I have some form of an "aura" about me but I say is nothing but The Spirit of The Living Lord being upon me as a truly sanctified child of The MOST High.

May you have a hunger so deep and the willingness to allow the Holy Spirit to work in you, with you and through you and allow Him to deposit all the 9 fruit (s) in your life. Be the light of this world radiating the presence of God Himself through every fibre of your being.

As I mentioned earlier, choose God's agenda and not your own and let the fruit (s) of His Holy Spirit give you the credibility, which matters in the eyes of Him, our Heavenly Father and not through the credibility applauded by man. Let the multitude of people get saved and may you serve as a witness to them through them seeing His Holy Spirit operating through you.

Step into all that our Heavenly Father has given us, let His fruits flow through you, which as a reminder to you, come directly from Him. Do not reject the manifestation of God's work through His Holy Spirit. Let us look at the example of Self-control as the last fruit mentioned above. When God begins His work in you to remove all the iniquities, the things which are not of Him in you and you choose to resist Him and instead opt to rely on your own version of self-control, He will not force you and He will leave you be until you remember the earlier statement "it starts with me" and seek Him again for His work to be completed in you.

Individually, we all have a joint role to play. Remember what I shared earlier, that The Holy Spirit is a gentleman, He never forces Himself on us, and He works with us in joint co-operation. Here is an example, in scripture we read how our Lord Jesus paved the way for Peter to walk on water through His power however Peter had his part to play, his role was to step out of the boat and start walking. It was at that point of walking that the power of our Heavenly Father manifested that allowed Peter to walk on water.

I always say, we serve a living God and I am a believer that through His Holy Spirit, He gives supernatural abilities to willing vessels on this earth to not only change but to be transformed and set apart for His Glory.

As our Lord and Saviour is coming back, I am a firm believer of that revelation, I pray if you too share the same belief that your priorities will change and you will place Our Heavenly Father as number 1 in your heart and that you will place Him at the core of everything you do. I also pray that you will be open to receive His Holy Spirit and allow Him to cleanse, purge and purify you.

As I come to a final close on this book, I bid you a happy and truly blessed walk with God through the Love of Christ and through the guidance of His Spirit. May the manifestation of the 9 fruit (s) of The Holy Spirit be so evident in your life and propel you to higher heights.

ABOUT THE AUTHOR

Rosemary is a multiple Award winner, Commercial & Residential Property Surveyor, Owner of Swanilenga (a registered and protected name / brand associated with all areas of her interests and projects in Book Publications, Property, Charity, Fashion & Media etc). Rosemary has other books in Paperback & Kindle which can be obtained from Amazon directly & through various international links including Barnes and Noble etc.

In 2012, Rosemary was on the front page of the Evening Standards' Newspaper as a nominee to carry the 2012 Olympic Torch. Formerly, Rosemary is a Beauty Queen at heart who has had the pleasure of being Zambia's reigning Queen in the UK for 3 years in 2003 then moving upwards & onwards as Zambia's envoy at Miss World 2004 (where she met Lionel Richie) and as a finale to her pageantry chapter; Miss Universe 2007 (where she met Donald Trump - 45th President of the United States of America).

In November 2007, she received a Royal invitation from Buckingham Palace by Her Majesty the Queen to attend a reception recognising those who had made a national contribution to life and painted a positive image to Africa. Also in attendance from the Royal family were; The Duke of Edinburgh, Prince Michael of Kent and other Princesses.

Rosemary's first book; **EMBRACING NUMBER 7** was published in January 2014. Copies of that book can be obtained from Amazon directly & through various international links including Barnes and Noble etc, also available in Kindle version.

www.ingramcontent.com/pod-product-compliance
Lightning Source LLC
Chambersburg PA
CBHW071925020426
42331CB00010B/2725